For Lex, Ginger, Bonny and everlasting George.

With thanks and love to an extraordinary
and inspirational teacher, Tony van der Meché.

Published in 2014 by Melbournestyle Books
155 Clarendon Street South Melbourne
Victoria 3205, Australia
www.melbournestyle.com.au
www.alphabet-city.com.au

National Library of Australia
Cataloguing-in-Publication entry:

Coote, Maree, author, illustrator.

Alphabet city zoo: making pictures with
the a-b-c / Maree Coote, author, illustrator.

ISBN 978-0-9924917-0-3   (hbk.)

1. English language – Alphabet – Juvenile literature
2. Animals – Pictorial works – Juvenile literature
3. Typography – Concrete poetry

421.1

Printed in China

10 9 8 7 6 5 4 3 2 1

MELBOURNESTYLE
AUSTRALIA

www.melbournestyle.com.au
www.alphabet-city.com.au

ALPHABET-CITY.COM.AU

ALPHABET CiTY Zoo

Making pictures with the A-B-C

Can you spell a kangaroo?

by
MAREE COOTE

Can you spell a kangaroo?
Yes, at Alphabet City Zoo!
Find the letters in the art,
It's easy once you make a start.
Spell a picture, not a word?
That's the craziest thing I've heard!
In a nutshell, here's the game:
Find the letters of my name.

In my portrait (so they tell me)
Hide the letters that will spell me:

{ m - o - N - k - e - y }

Sometimes letters might repeat,
To make more eyes or hands or feet,
But all the letters can be found,
Back-to-front or upside-down.
Spell each creature, find its name,
That's the alphabetical game.

Can you spell a kangaroo?

Yes, and baby joey too!

Can you find these letters in the picture?

KANGAROo + Joey

Can you
spell a
crocodile?

Yes!
But it may
take
a while...

Can you find these letters in the picture?

Can you spell an elephant?

Yes.
I bet you think I can't.

Can you find these letters in the picture?

Could
you
spell a
tiger too?

Shouldn't
be too hard
to do...

Can you find these letters in the picture?

tigeR

You couldn't spell a panda, though?

I'm prepared to have a go.

Can you find these letters in the picture?

Can you spell a hissing snake?

Yes. Let's see how long I take...

Can you find these letters in the picture?

SNAKe

Can you spell an emu, too?

Just three letters? Hard to do!

Can you find these letters in the picture?

Can you spell koala bear?

(It's not a bear), but here's a pair.

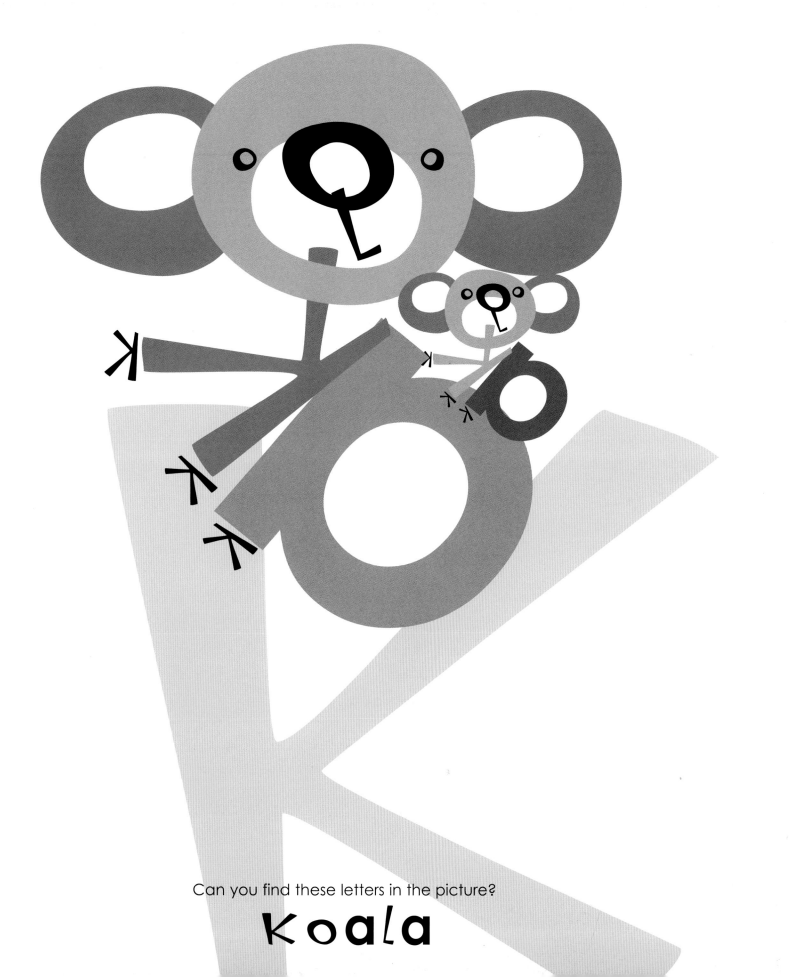

Can you find these letters in the picture?

Koala

Could you spell a zebra then?

I could spell one; I could spell ten.

Can you find these letters in the picture?

Zebra

Can you spell a lion now?

Yes, and I can show you how.

Can you find these letters in the picture?

What
about
a
lioness?

Absolutely.
Sure can.
Yes.

Can you find these letters in the picture?

LIONESS

Can you spell me a giraffe?

Certainly! Don't make me laugh!

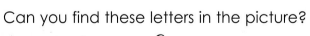

Can you find these letters in the picture?

Can you
spell
a gibbon
too?

Anything
that's in
the zoo!

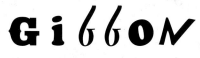

Can you find these letters in the picture?

Gibbon

Anything that's in the zoo?

Anything! Yes! Even YOU!

Can you find these letters in the picture?

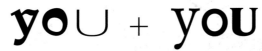